The Battle of Dunnichen

The Battle of Dunnichen

An account of the Pictish victory
at the Battle of Dunnichen, also known
as Nechtansmere, fought on
the 20th of May 685

With an Appendix
The Dunnichen Stone

GRAEME CRUICKSHANK
MA, AMA, FMA, FSA Scot

The Pinkfoot Press
Balgavies, Angus
1999

Published in Scotland by
The Pinkfoot Press
Balgavies, Forfar, Angus DD8 2TH

First edition 1991
Reprinted 1992
Second edition 1999

(First published 1985 by Forfar and
District Historical Society, entitled:
Nechtansmere 1300: a Commemoration)

ISBN 1 874012 23 7

Produced and designed at The Pinkfoot Press
Printed by Burns Harris and Findlay Ltd, Dundee

Contents

Illustrations

Initials *b* and *d* in the cover title are from
the MS 'Fragmentary Irish Annals' by
Duald MacFirbis, as are the labels *bruide*
(p.41) and *mc Ossa rí Saxan* ('son of
Oswiu king of the Saxons') (p.44)

Details from the battle-scene on the
Aberlemno Churchyard Stone:

Pictish and Northumbrian
cavalrymen in combat *front cover*
Pictish infantry *opp. title*
Northumbrian leader (?Ecgfrith) 15
Northumbrian cavalryman 20
Pictish leader (?Bruide) 4, 41
Northumbrian corpse (?Ecgfrith)
pecked by carrion bird 44

Acknowledgements

The author and publishers wish to thank
the following who have kindly permitted
reproduction of their photographs:
Royal Library of Albert I, Brussels (**4**);
the late Dr Gordon Burgess (**5** – also
used as a basis for the illustrated details);
Mrs Barbara Lees, widow of Dr Frederick
Wainwright (**8**); Kim Cessford (**9**)

Foreword

'This day Bruide fights a battle for the heritage of his grandfather'

The compelling certainty of knowing that 'this day' was the 20th of May 685, contrasts sharply with the other surviving evidence of the Battle of Dunnichen. Nevertheless, Graeme Cruickshank has carefully assembled and examined this evidence and his conclusions provide a vivid narrative of the events leading up to the battle, a dramatic account of the battle itself, an assessment of the consequences of the Pictish victory and the relevance of this historic watershed to the present time.

It is almost solely due to the author's infectious enthusiasm for his subject that Dunnichen is now firmly established on the itinerary of all latter-day Pictish pilgrims. However, an unforeseen consequence of the popularisation of the battle was an annual invasion in May of new-age travellers who adopted Dunnichen Hill as the site for a music festival. This created a lot of official hostility resulting in police action against the revellers, and headlines about the 'new battle of Dunnichen'. The local authority now holds the upper hand, having thwarted the enterprise by imposing a five-mile exclusion zone around the hill.

Since the last edition of this booklet was published, plans to establish a quarry on West Dunnichen Hill have been refused, but a local opposition group remains prepared to counter any further threatening application. Scott Kidd of Letham was the instigator and chairman of the successful Save Dunnichen Hill Campaign and he worked tirelessly on its behalf. Sadly he died last year, but he has been fittingly commemorated by the erection of a cairn beside the footpath from Dunnichen to Letham on the south side of Dunnichen Moss. The memorial overlooks the spot where now the former Mire has reappeared in miniature, the farmer of East Mains of Dunnichen having excavated a pool at its old centre.

Finally, the Dunnichen Stone (see Appendix p.45), which has suffered a rather chequered recent history, is now happily restored to its original neighbourhood, where it is on display in the Meffan Institute, Forfar.

1991 (revised 1999)   David Henry

Introduction

At around three o'clock in the afternoon of Saturday 20th May 685, close to the present hamlet of Dunnichen in Angus (near Letham, some three miles south-east of Forfar), there occurred one of the most crucial battles in the Dark Age history of Britain. The contestants were the forces of the Picts, under king Bruide (this being one of several ways in which his name may be spelt), and the invading Northumbrians, under king Ecgfrith, with the Picts emerging victorious in a most decisive fashion. There are indications that they owed their success both to a cleverly-devised strategy in determining the field of battle, and to their well-rehearsed and disciplined tactics once the enemy was engaged.

It seems likely that the topography around Dunnichen was crucial to the success of the Pictish battle-plan. One element was Dunnichen Hill, which may have accommodated the stronghold of Dun Nechtan (the hill-fort of king Nechtan). The other was an area of water and swamp which may have been known as Nechtan's Mire. It occupied the shallow valley lying at the foot of the Hill on its southern side, and was latterly called Dunnichen Moss. Agricultural improvements of the 19th and 20th centuries have greatly altered, though not entirely obliterated, this feature.

The Pictish victory at Dunnichen was of immense importance. It seems to represent a united effort by the Pictish peoples, and much lost territory was recovered. The Northumbrians were pushed back south of the Firth of Forth, and they never regained their former power. Most significantly of all, it paved the way for northern Britain to become the independent nation of Scotland and not merely an extension of England. Most books on Scottish history mention the Battle of Dunnichen (generally calling it by its English name of Nechtansmere), but usually they do so only fleetingly.

The celebrations which took place in 1985 commemorating the 1300th anniversary of the Battle provided an appropriate occasion to indulge in a detailed reappraisal of this important event. This author was commissioned by the Forfar and District Historical Society to write a booklet on the subject which is now out of print. A fuller version complete with references is in the course of preparation, but is still some way from completion. This volume began as a second edition of the original booklet – *Nechtansmere 1300: a Commemoration* – but contains a great many amendments, and several passages have been completely rewritten and new ones added. I would like to thank David Henry of the Pinkfoot Press, which is located less than two miles from Dunnichen Hill, for his initiative in publishing it at this time of renewed interest in the Battle and its historical significance.

Edinburgh, June 1991   GDRC

APOLOGIA

In the first version of this booklet, published in 1985 to commemorate the battle, I added a little note at the end which concluded: 'A fuller version, including references and acknowledgements, is currently in the course of preparation.' It may be regarded as something of a disappointment that more than a dozen years later, that promise remains unfulfilled.

The first one-third of the larger work, which will comprise 33 chapters in all, was written in 1988 (during a four-month sojourn in the mountain country of Papua New Guinea), following which one chapter was developed into a full-scale book, *The Aberlemno Battle-Scene*, soon to be published by the Pinkfoot Press.

Then, in 1990, I embarked upon a project which has dominated my life since – locating and recording examples of antique Scottish pottery which were exported to South-East Asia. Writing up the results is now well under way. After publication, I intend to return to the task of completing *The Battle of Dunnichen* book, replete with all the references which are still absent from this summary.

Edinburgh, May 1999   GDRC

1 Historical Background

The key to the conflict between the Picts and the Northumbrians, which reached its climax at the Battle of Dunnichen, lay in the disappearance of Gododdin. This was the name of the territory, and also of the people who occupied it, which lay in the area of what eventually became south-east Scotland. It consisted of all of the Lothians, extending south at least to the Lammermuir Hills, and perhaps even to the Tweed, and it included the district of Manau to the west (the Stirling/Clackmannan area). By the beginning of the 7th century, Gododdin was showing signs of decline, though it did manage to survive a major catastrophe around the year 600 when its warband ('army' seems too grand a term for a mere three hundred warriors) marched heroically out of *Din Eidyn* (Edinburgh) and into Northumbrian territory, only to be almost totally annihilated at *Catreath* (Catterick). Their brave venture was the subject of the oldest surviving Scottish poem. It contains references to two or three warriors who may have been Picts, and if so, it would indicate a Pictish martial involvement against the Northumbrians which was to foreshadow the massive military conflicts between the two powers which were to dominate much of the history of northern Britain in the 7th century.

With Gododdin on the wane, the question was which of its neighbours would move in and annex the territory. The cousins of the Gododdin, the Britons of Strathclyde, were pinned back by the remorseless Northumbrian advance in the west. Alarmed by this, the Scots of Dalriada marched to repel them, but were decisively defeated at the Battle of Degsastan in 603. This left the Northumbrians as the obvious power to move into the vacuum created by the collapse of Gododdin. Even so, they moved cautiously, taking several decades to capture the key strongholds, the siege and fall of *Din Eidyn* in 638 doubtless marking the extinction of Gododdin. Its western extension of Manau may have held out a little longer, but was under Northumbrian control by the middle of the century.

This meant that the Picts and the Northumbrians now had some form of common border: they would have faced each other across the Firth of Forth, and they would have been even closer upriver in the Stirling area.

Warfare was inevitable – but not immediate. The reason, at least in part, was the blood relationship which existed between one royal lineage of the Picts and that of the Northumbrians. It was caused by events which occurred in the aftermath of the death of Aethelfrith, king of Northumbria, in 616. He had united Bernicia and Deira into one kingdom, though it was an uneasy union. Although he had three sons, his successor was Edwin of Deira, who assumed the throne by conquest, and as the young heirs were Bernician, it was deemed expedient to remove them swiftly out of harm's way. Surprising though it may seem considering their hostility later in the century, the Northumbrian refugees sought safety in Pictland.

It seems that the two elder brothers, Oswald and Oswiu, may have then gone to live with the Scots, but the youngest, Eanfrith, who was only an infant at the time, remained with the Picts, where he grew to maturity and married a lady of a Pictish royal house. This prestigious dynastic marriage had a very important result: if, as is generally supposed, the succession of the Pictish kingship was matrilinear (*ie* through the female line), it meant that a son of this Northumbrian prince could become a Pictish king, and so indeed it transpired.

Around 632 Edwin of Northumbria was killed by Cadwallon, king of Gwynedd in north Wales, and Aethelfrith's three sons returned to their homeland. Eanfrith, although the youngest, assumed the crown, at least in Bernicia – but only for a matter of months, for he was murdered when he went to Cadwallon to arrange a peace. This meant that the prospect of kings of Northumbria and Pictland who were father and son ruling simultaneously would not materialise. The two remaining brothers then ruled Northumbria successively for almost forty years. Oswald reunited Bernicia and Deira into a single kingdom once more, an expanding kingdom hungry for conquest. When the third brother, Oswiu, came to the throne in 642, Gododdin was already in effect part of Northumbria. The next step would involve a clash with the Picts, and Northumbrian aggression was soon set on a course which was to culminate more than four decades later at Dunnichen.

Oswiu of Northumbria certainly had designs on the territory of the Picts, but for a time much of his attention was occupied in dealing with a threat on his southern border from the kingdom of Mercia. Even so, it seems likely that some Pictish territory, especially in the area north of Manau, was annexed by Northumbria. As the place-name evidence

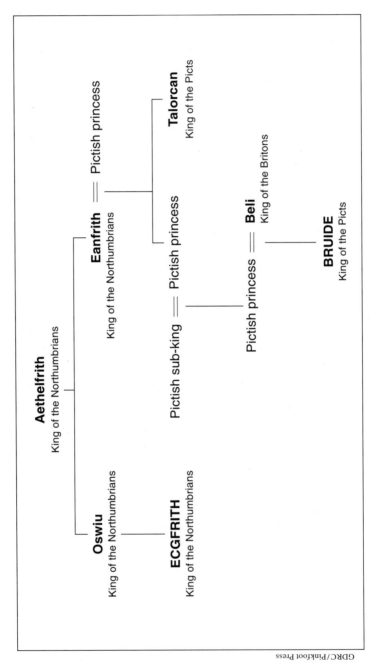

Aethelfrith
King of the Northumbrians

Oswiu
King of the Northumbrians

Eanfrith = Pictish princess
King of the Northumbrians

ECGFRITH
King of the Northumbrians

Talorcan
King of the Picts

Pictish sub-king = Pictish princess

Pictish princess = **Beli**
King of the Britons

BRUIDE
King of the Picts

1 Kinship chart *The chart shows the relationship between Bruide and Ecgfrith. It is correct as far as the grandsons of Aethelfrith; after that, the Pictish descent is uncertain, this chart being based on the best evidence currently available. A Pictish 'princess' should not be equated with the daughter of a king, the term as used here merely indicating a lady of a Pictish royal house.*

suggests that some Pictish settlement had taken place south of the Forth prior to the Northumbrian advance, the Picts can have had no doubt about the Northumbrian policy of aggressive territorial expansion. When Oswiu finally defeated and killed Penda of Mercia at the battle of Winwaed in 655, he was free to devote all his energy to a determined incursion into Pictland.

It was now that the link between the Northumbrian and Pictish dynasties came into play. It will be remembered that while he was exiled in Pictland, Eanfrith of Northumbria had married a Pictish princess; their son, Talorcan, was soon to become king of the Picts. It would seem that for a couple of years prior to 655, the Picts were without a king, an unsettled position which must have ideally suited Oswiu. He was of course the uncle of Talorcan, and his influence must have been considerable. It is likely that he assisted Talorcan to gain the throne in 658, and supported him in his victory over the Scots about that time. Northumbria thus gained a measure of control over Pictland, but Talorcan died in 662, and during the remaining eight years of Oswiu's reign, such understandings may well have turned into resented obligations. Even so, there would seem to have been no major military clashes between the Picts and Northumbrians at this time, which points to the strong suspicion that Talorcan's successors, the brothers Gartnait and Drest, sons of Donuel, were also placed on the throne at Oswiu's instigation, and made to rule successively for at least a decade as Northumbrian puppet-kings.

There can be no doubt that a sizeable part of Pictland lay under Northumbrian control. Bede records that 'Oswiu subjected the greater part of the Pictish race to the dominion of the English', though it did have its limits, for Bede also describes Bishop Wilfrid as 'administering the see of the church of York and of all the Northumbrians and Picts, as far as Oswiu was able to extend his power'. Just what form this took is uncertain; it may have been military occupation, or simply the exaction of tribute perhaps backed up by the holding of hostages. Whatever it was, the southern Picts had become an oppressed people. Nor were they alone, for the Britons of Strathclyde had been in a similar position for some time, and the Scots of Dalriada were also in like circumstances. The power of Northumbria appeared to grow unchallenged throughout northern Britain.

This was to change dramatically after the death of Oswiu in 670. He was succeeded by his son, Ecgfrith, though it seems that there was an initial period of readjustment before the new king assumed full control. Although we have no details, it would appear that the Picts took advantage of the brief unsettling effect of the change in Northumbrian leadership to make an attempt 'to throw off the yoke of slavery', as it was expressed a few years later by Eddius Stephanus. It is doubtful if this involved actual rebellion; more likely it was a show of strength coupled with bold words. It is not known which Pictish king was on the throne at this moment; if it was still Drest, the Northumbrian vassal, this may have been the time when he was driven out, and Bruide put in his place, with the declared aim of restoring independence. Whatever the precise nature of the Pictish initiative, it infuriated Ecgfrith, who reacted in swift and terrible fashion.

According to the account given by Eddius, news reached Ecgfrith that the Picts were gathering from the north in force, and he decided to forestall any planned rebellion by making a pre-emptive strike against them. He quickly gathered an army of horsemen (this being the earliest-known mention of cavalry in English history), and attacked the Picts with ruthless ferocity, so that an enormous number of them were slain. The gruesome account says that two rivers were filled with the corpses of the Pictish dead, so that the Northumbrians were able to cross over dry-shod to pursue and kill great numbers of the fugitives. These two rivers were probably the Avon and the Carron; they only get close when they flow into the Firth of Forth, being separated there by less than two miles (the land where Grangemouth now stands). This battle took place between 670 and 675, probably around 672. The Northumbrian army, having made slaughter far and wide, returned laden with spoil.

Thus the Picts in the area of Northumbrian control were again reduced to a state of slavery, in which they were to remain until the tables were turned more than a dozen years later at Dunnichen. It may be wondered why it took the Picts so long to attempt to avenge such a horrendous defeat and regain their freedom. For a start, recovering from such appalling losses would have been a slow process. Moreover, the new king, Bruide (the third Pictish king of that name), would have taken time to establish himself. Had Drest still been on the throne at the time of the battle, its result would surely have led to his expulsion (which occurred about this time), and Bruide's first task would have been to restore some measure of confidence among his shattered people. On the other hand, if Drest had already been expelled, and Bruide had led the Picts to such a disastrous defeat, he would have had the additional problem of re-establishing his own credibility as a military leader.

Either way, the task which faced Bruide was immense, and it is small wonder that it took him a dozen years to achieve it. We know little of how this was done, but it is likely that the remaining years of the 670s formed a period of recuperation, while during the early 680s Bruide set about establishing his authority throughout the lands of the Picts in readiness for the great test against the Northumbrians. Irish sources give brief hints of how this objective was pursued: the 'Annals of Ulster' record the siege of Dunnottar in 681, and the 'Annals of Tigernach' speak of the destruction of the Orkneys in 682. Although the latter entry contains the only direct mention of Bruide in relation to these various actions, it seems unlikely that this was the only one in which he was involved. It could be that the victory at Dunnichen amounted to the culmination of his campaigning – the objective which all his efforts had been dedicated to achieve.

It seems likely that by 685, Pictland formed a single kingdom, and it is virtually certain that Bruide was recognised as king by all the Picts. Nothing has been recorded to indicate the reasons which impelled Ecgfrith to invade Pictland at this time, but it may well have been the same type of circumstances which had prevailed a dozen years earlier. If Bruide, secure in his leadership of the Picts, had started massing his forces on the boundary of Northumbrian-controlled Pictland, and if he had made his intention clear at some parley by expressing sentiments along the lines of 'Northumbrians go home – or else…', backed up by guerilla-type raids to demonstrate that he was not bluffing, then Ecgfrith's martial tendency would doubtless have led to his raising an army and marching north to crush such rebellious notions. He would have been in no doubt that his devastating triumph of 672 could be repeated in 685, thereby keeping the southern Picts in a state of subjugation for another dozen years at least, and perhaps adding to that part of Pictland already under Northumbrian domination.

During his fifteen years as king of the Northumbrians, Ecgfrith had established a considerable reputation as a military leader, even though he did not always emerge as victor (he had, for instance, been decisively beaten by the Mercians in 679). Nevertheless, he must have been in confident mood in 685, for in the previous year his troops had waged a successful war in Ireland, where they had encountered little difficulty in wasting the province of Brega. The Pictish king, too, had reason to feel confident of the outcome of an encounter with the Northumbrians. So it was that in the late spring of 685, Ecgfrith led the Northumbrian army north to do battle with the Picts under their king, Bruide.

It is curious, considering the gulf of antagonism between the Picts and the Northumbrians, and the hostility which had existed for several decades, that the two kings were related to each other, having a common ancestor in Aethelfrith of Northumbria. Ecgfrith was his grandson; another grandson was Talorcan, a previous Pictish king, son of Eanfrith who had been exiled for a period in Pictland and married a Pictish princess. The remaining relationship pattern on the Pictish side is somewhat uncertain, and although Bruide and Ecgfrith are referred to as cousins by Nennius in his 'Historia Brittonum', the term was probably meant to indicate a less precise kinship. Illustration 1 (p.10), which is based on the best evidence available, shows that Bruide was the second-grand-nephew of Ecgfrith.

The two armies met in a mighty battle, though very few details relating to it have come down to us. One of the principal questions, the actual location where the conflict occurred, has been the subject of much historical debate, and it is fair to say that its precise whereabouts are still not known as a matter of factual certainty. Indeed, arguments can be put forward in favour of various locations. The problem is simply a lack of surviving evidence, which means that historians can do no more than examine such scraps as exist, and attempt to make reasoned deductions from them. The Picts themselves have left us nothing in the way of written records which can be of assistance, and we must rely on the writings of English monks and the compilers of the Irish annals.

By far the most valuable source is Bede's 'Historia Ecclesiastica', not only because (despite its brevity) it is the most extensive account we have, but also because it was written by a historian who was alive at the time of the battle. Bede records that in 685, Ecgfrith rashly led his army to ravage a province of the Picts, against the advice of his friends, particularly Bishop Cuthbert. When he encountered the Pictish forces, they feigned flight, and lured him into the defiles of inaccessible mountains, where the contest was decided. The implication is that Ecgfrith penetrated beyond the limit of Northumbrian-controlled Pictland, which most likely would have involved marching north of the Tay. The topographical description sounds as if it refers to the Grampian Mountains, though Bede is only going on a second-hand account, and probably a Northumbrian one at that (though he may have had the benefit of more than one source). Scottish mountains of even modest proportions might have appeared impressive to the invaders, and any Northumbrian version of events would have had a vested interest in portraying the terrain as being alien and unfavourable to their troops.

Surprisingly (and for the sake of historians, disappointingly) Bede does not name this momentous battle, but two other sources give it a name of sorts, which provide clues to its location. Three Irish annals call it the *Battle of Duin Ne(a)chtain*, which may be equated with Dun Nechtan (the hill-fort of Nechtan), and the name has survived to the present time as Dunnichen, in Angus. The other link with Nechtan occurs in the English name for the battle – *Nechtan's Mere*, of which the earliest surviving reference is that of Symeon of Durham in the early 12th century, though he was undoubtedly drawing upon earlier Northumbrian sources. As this is the only known reference to such a geographical feature, it seems reasonable to locate this mire in the neighbourhood of Dun Nechtan, which leads us again to Dunnichen as the likely site of the battle. Another morsel of evidence which supports this proposition is the name given by Nennius in his 'History of the Britons', where it is called *Gueith Linn Garan*. This has been translated as 'The Battle of the Pool of the Heron', which contains a watery element similar to that of the English name.

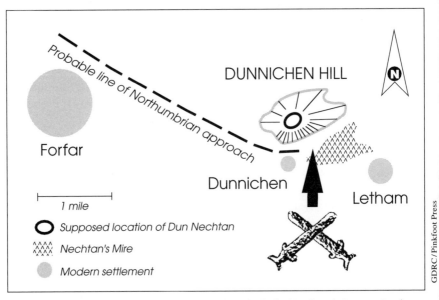

2 Line of approach *The likely route by which the Northumbrians arrived at Dunnichen*

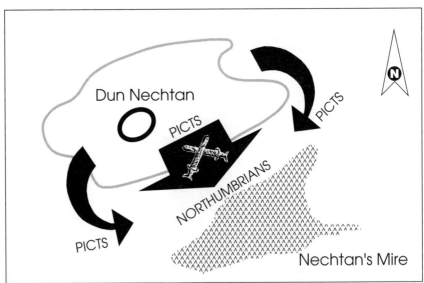

3 Deployment of forces *Showing the tactics which the Picts may have employed to spring the trap and defeat their enemy.*

2 Conduct of the Battle

If we accept Dunnichen as the site of the battle, we can then put together an account of the Northumbrian invasion with some measure of confidence that it may be reasonably accurate. Ecgfrith would have set out at the head of his army in the spring of 685, doubtless taking the east-coast route through the former territory of Gododdin, marching by way of the strongholds captured by his forebears earlier in the century. He probably stopped for a while at *Din Eidyn* (Edinburgh) to make final preparations for the incursion into Pictland. The assumption is that he continued northwards through and beyond the area of southern Pictland under his control, moving inland to negotiate the firths, which probably meant crossing the Forth near Stirling and the Tay near Perth. From such a position, there would have been two options: either to head north-east up Strathmore between the ranges of the Grampians and the Sidlaws, or to take a parallel but more southerly route along the Carse of Gowrie between the Sidlaws and the Tay estuary. Either could lead to Dunnichen, though the former would do so more readily, and would avoid the danger of the Northumbrians being trapped with the sea at their backs, or having the line of their retreat cut off at Perth. Moreover, Strathmore provided a better natural way for an army on the march.

Having got Ecgfrith and his army marching purposefully up Strathmore, we must now account for him deviating from his route, presumably just north of Forfar, and heading for Dunnichen. At this point, it is worth recalling the words of Bede: the Picts feigned flight, and lured the Northumbrians into mountainous country. Up until now, we have been considering the campaign from the standpoint of Ecgfrith; we should now turn our thoughts to how Bruide viewed the invasion. Whether or not he had been on the throne at the time of the previous battle with the Northumbrians, that of *circa* 672, the full horror of that devastating defeat must have had a profound effect upon him, either as a new king suffering a humiliating disaster at the start of his reign, or as the next in line who came to the throne in the wake of that terrible catastrophe. Either way, Bruide would want to make sure that not only was he ready to take on

Ecgfrith, but that the mistakes of the previous encounter would not be repeated. It is reasonable to suppose that the Picts had a plan to bring them victory.

The earlier battle had been fought on flat land, where large armies could be marshalled and deployed. Bruide's strategy was apparently to force the Northumbrians to fight on **his** choice of territory, which was rather different. To achieve this, he employed the simple and oft-used tactic of showing a small part of his force to the enemy, and then pretending to run from them, drawing them after in pursuit in hope of an easy victory. The idea would then be to lure the enemy into an ambush, making full use of the local topography to entrap them and help secure their defeat.

So why did Ecgfrith fall for such an obvious ruse? Most historians seem to have assumed that because the scant records make no mention of hostilities between the Pictish and Northumbrian armies prior to their encounter at Dunnichen, this meant that Ecgfrith's advance was unopposed. This hardly seems likely, for much of Pictland was cloaked in dense forest, which would have provided excellent cover for the sniping activities of Pictish archers. Under such circumstances, it would hardly be surprising if Ecgfrith was angered and frustrated at having his army harassed and whittled down by the hand of an unseen foe, so that when he at last caught sight of the enemy, he ordered his men to attack them. The apparent Pictish flight would have served to give impetus to the Northumbrian charge.

If this was Bruide's plan, it was working well so far, but the trap still had to be sprung. For success to be achieved, it was necessary for Ecgfrith to approach Dunnichen from a north or westerly direction. An approach from the south would have afforded a clear view of the forbidding form of Dun Nechtan, while coming from the east would have meant an encounter with Nechtan's Mire, either of which would have caused the Northumbrians to hang back. From the little we know, it would appear that they continued their pursuit, and so we may surmise that they approached Dunnichen from a north-westerly direction, skirting the base of the hill on its western and southern sides (**2**). What happened then (as indicated diagrammatically in illus.**3**) is pure conjecture, but it may be reasonable to speculate that when the Northumbrians burst through the defile where the modern village of Dunnichen now stands, they found the

Picts, whom they had imagined to be in full flight, standing firm before them. Too late, they saw with dread the ramparts of Dun Nechtan looming above them. A detachment of Picts from the fort swiftly barred the path of their retreat, while the main Pictish host gathered on the brow of the hill, preparing for the onslaught. On their only open side lay the pool and marshland which for many of them would soon become a watery grave. The trap could now be sprung.

Such a description of the battle is speculative, but it does take account of the local topography, and it represents both the hill-fort and the mire as important factors in the successful outcome of the Pictish victory, which accords with the names given to the engagement in the Irish annals, and an English chronicle, respectively. What we do know (every source of information about the battle stating it), is that the Northumbrians were routed, the majority of their forces, including king Ecgfrith himself, being slain. Bede adds the detail that the royal bodyguard died to a man, vainly fighting to protect their beleaguered monarch. Of the survivors, of which there were not many, most were enslaved by the Picts; only a few struggled back home to break the awesome news to their people.

The Battle of Dunnichen represents a mighty clash of arms which can have had few equals in the history of Dark-Age Britain. No indication whatsoever has come down to us regarding the size of the respective armies, but there is little doubt that they would have consisted of the maximum potency which each side could muster. Ecgfrith is hardly likely to have embarked upon such an invasion without the full weight of his military resources, while Bruide must have realised that to repulse an attack of that scale (which he himself may have initiated) would require the deployment of all the martial power that Pictland could summon together. Despite so many uncertainties about the battle, we know one important fact about it with an astonishing degree of accuracy – **when** it was fought. By drawing together a number of references, not all of them relating directly to the battle, it can be stated with confidence that the Battle of Dunnichen took place at around three o'clock in the afternoon of Saturday, 20th May, in the year 685.

By contrast, doubt surrounds another important feature of the battle, and that is **what** it should be called. As it was fought in Pictish territory, and the Picts were the victors, their name should be the one we use, but they have left no written record of the battle. Our chief source of primary information, Bede, gives no name to the conflict, and so we must rely on the brief entries in later compilations. As mentioned above, three Irish annals call it the Battle of Dun Nechtan, this name coming by way of the Scots of Dalriada. These three annals – the ' Annals of Ulster', the 'Annals of Tigernach' and the 'Fragmentary Irish Annals' – have variations in the form of the name, but they all coincide in translation. In the tradition of naming a battle after the place where it was fought, the 'Battle of Dunnichen' would seem to suit very well. It is the English name of Nechtansmere, however, which has been commonly used. It first appears in a history of the early 12th century by Symeon of Durham, and may well be what the Northumbrians called it at the time. Had it been fought somewhat later in history, both these elements could have been combined in a name such as 'The Battle of Dunnichen Moss', for the map evidence illustrates that this is what Nechtan's Mire was commonly called in more recent times. There is, however, a third contender for the name, which comes from the 'Historia Brittonum' of Nennius, where the conflict is called the Battle of Linn Garan. This seems to have come by way of the Britons of Strathclyde, and may be close to, or even the same as, the name which the Picts themselves gave to the battle. It is curious that of the three candidates, Dunnichen is the most appropriate, and Linn Garan is the most authentic, yet it is the hybrid Nechtansmere which appears in most history books. It is hardly logical to call a battle by the name by which it was known to the vanquished, especially if part of that name is alien to local usage. It is only sensible that this conflict be termed the Battle of Dunnichen; this accords with modern local preference, and, increasingly, with academic opinion.

3 Results of the Battle

The outcome of the Battle of Dunnichen had far-reaching consequences, not only for the Picts and the Northumbrians, but also for their neighbours, and for the future of northern Britain in terms of the development into nationhood of Scotland and England. For the Picts, the greatest of all their victories brought freedom from Northumbrian domination, both actual and threatened. The enemy was driven entirely from Pictland, and whether there had been a physical occupation, a tribute system, or a combination of the two, it was now at an end. The Picts re-established the Firth of Forth as their southern boundary, and there is some suggestion by later writers such as William of Malmesbury that they went beyond it; John of Tynemouth, writing in the mid-14th century, indicates that it extended as far as the Tweed. It is likely that the Picts followed up their success by raiding into Northumbria, and may have occupied the northern part for a time, but it seems that both sides came to regard the Forth as the permanent boundary between them.

Bede records that 'the Picts recovered their own land which the English had formerly held', which strengthens the theory of an occupied territory in southern Pictland; Nennius relates that the Northumbrians 'never again were allowed to exact a tax from the Picts', which gives credence to the tribute theory, though whether for the same or different areas we cannot say. Thus all the incursions of the Northumbrians, effected during the previous thirty years by dynastic, political, and military means, were brought to nought. It was not only the Picts who benefited, but also the Scots of Dalriada and the Britons of Strathclyde; they too had been under some form of Northumbrian domination, and now, according to Bede, they recovered their independence.

The power of Northumbria, and the policy of aggressive expansion which it nurtured, had been checked – permanently, as it turned out – but it had not been broken, and it is something of an irony that, as kingdoms go, Northumbria was to outlast Pictland by several decades. Nor was war ended between the two, for there were to be several more major battles between them, with mixed results. A clash in 698 seems to have given the Picts another victory, though in 711 it was the Northumbrians who triumphed on the Plain of Manau, the scene of their devastating success of half a century earlier. Perhaps when the Pictish king Nechtan sent a letter to Abbot Ceolfrith of Jarrow in about 715 asking advice on certain matters of Christian doctrine, he was actually making an overture for the establishment of a state of peaceful coexistence.

The political and territorial consequences of the battle provided the most important results, but there was another sphere of interest which must not be overlooked – that of religion. It would seem that the Northumbrian church was just as expansionist as its kings and secular leaders. The writings of Eddius Stephanus make it clear that while Ecgfrith was zealous in his efforts to extend his kingdom in all directions, Bishop Wilfrid took advantage of this (before he fell from favour) and did likewise in a religious context, and the Picts are mentioned among those peoples brought within his 'ecclesiastical kingdom'. When Theodore, Archbishop of York, set about reorganising the northern English church in 678, he created a number of new sees, including that of *Aebbercurnig* (Abercorn in West Lothian), which was established in 681.

The bishop appointed to Abercorn was Trumwine, who was a cleric of some standing, as indicated by the call he received three years later to accompany Ecgfrith on his important and delicate mission out to the Great Farne in order to persuade Cuthbert to become Bishop of Lindisfarne. Trumwine was sent, according to Bede, *ad provinciam Pictorum* (to a province of the Picts), and this has been taken to mean one of the seven provinces of Pictland, the most likely contender being *Fib* (Fife and Kinross). However, the precise geographical extent of this diocese is not known, and if religion echoed political and military territoriality, then it could have extended throughout the whole area of southern Pictland which lay under Northumbrian control. It might even, with missionary zeal, have been taken further, in which case the roles would have been reversed, with religion succeeding where force of arms had not yet triumphed in the spreading of Northumbrian influence.

The monastery of *Aebbercurnig*, which was Trumwine's head-quarters, was situated some three miles west of the modern burgh of Queensferry. It may seem odd that if Trumwine had been sent as bishop to the Picts, he should have his base south of the Firth of Forth, when all the evidence points to Northumbrian control being solidly established for a long way north of it. The solution may be that Trumwine had a two-fold mission: to cater for the spiritual needs of those south of the Forth in what Bede termed 'the English region', *ie* the northernmost part of Northumbria proper, and also to bring within his flock those to the north of the Forth for as far as it was practical to go.

The Pictish victory at Dunnichen put an end to all that. Bishop Trumwine was apparently in Pictland at the time of the battle, and he fled with such haste that it is reported that he did not break his journey until he had gone as far as Whitby. The see of Abercorn was abandoned, and never revived. However, the new situation did not endure for very long, for some thirty years later Nechtan, after consultation with the Northumbrian clergy, decided to abandon the traditional practices of Columban Christianity and come within the fold of orthodox Roman teaching. If this was a part of Ecgfrith's reason for invading Pictland, then the Battle of Dunnichen had delayed his objective by a mere three decades; in military and political terms, however, the results of their triumph were to remain with the Picts.

If Bruide indeed had a plan to achieve victory over the Northumbrians, it is reasonable to suppose that he also had a series of objectives in mind should he gain the victory. Of course, it can be no more than unverifiable speculation, but in practical terms, he may have formulated these five aims: to avenge the horrendous defeat by the Northumbrians of *circa* 672; to prevent any more of Pictland falling under Northumbrian control; to liberate that part of Pictland which had already come under Northumbrian domination; to place a permanent check upon the Northumbrian policy of territorial expansion at the expense of Pictland; and to establish a southern boundary which would not be subject to the threat of continued Northumbrian aggression. It may be reckoned that Bruide scored four and a half out of five, and considering the scale of the battle, a success rating in the region of 90% must represent a major achievement. The consequences of this success were vital for the future nationhood of Scotland.

4 The Dunnichen victory song *Part of a manuscript entitled 'Fragmentary Irish Annals', copied from ancient sources by Duald MacFirbis (MS5301, fol30). The verse about the Battle of Dunnichen is at the bottom; the name 'bruide' appears in the first and last lines.*

24

4 Relics of the Battle

It is a matter of lasting sorrow that the Picts left no written records which tell of their feelings about the Battle of Dunnichen: how they viewed the significance of their victory, and the way they celebrated the devastating manner of its achievement. There is, however, a fragment of verse relating to the battle which may be contemporary, and which, although not written by a Pict, could have been written in Pictland (**4**). It appears to be part of a song of victory in commemoration of the battle and of the victorious king. The six lines of verse have been preserved in a document known as the 'Fragmentary Irish Annals', copied from ancient sources by Duald MacFirbis. It is a curious compilation, apparently based as much on legend as on historical fact, and the date of the sources from which these fragments were copied is unknown. The Dunnichen verse is credited to Riaguil of Bennchor, an Irish cleric who was seemingly in Pictland at the time of the battle.

Confusingly, the verse does not appear in its correct chronological position, being mistakenly linked to the death not of Ecgfrith, but of his half-brother and successor, Aldfrith, whom it calls by his Irish name of Flainn Fiona. The error would not have been difficult to make, both men being sons of Oswiu. The introduction to the verse does not mention the vanquished king by name, merely calling him 'son of Oswiu, king of the Saxons', nor does it relate the name of the battle – even though a little earlier, in its correct position, the Battle of Duin Neachtain is listed, with Bruide mac Beli given as the victor. There is little doubt that the verse refers to the Battle of Dunnichen, for 'Bruide the brave' wins the day. Scholars are not generally agreed on a translation, but it may read something like this:

> *This day Bruide fights a battle*
> > *for the heritage of his grandfather,*
> *Unless the son of God wills it otherwise,*
> > *he will die in it;*
> *This day the son of Oswiu has been struck down*
> > *in a battle against blue swords,*

Although he has spoken penitence,
it is penitence too late;
This day the son of Oswiu has been struck down,
who had the black draughts,
Christ heard our supplications,
they spared Bruide the brave.

This verse may be only six lines in length, but it contains a number of enigmas and uncertainties. The Northumbrians fought 'against blue swords', implying that only the Picts possessed such weapons, and that there was something special about them. Ecgfrith 'had the black draughts' – this may mean that he had been given some form of poison, possibly polluted water, or perhaps in more sinister terms, he had deliberately taken such a draught (the drinking of black moss water was regarded in later times as evidence of consorting with the devil).

It is the first line which carries the greatest significance, however, for it has Bruide fighting a battle, or perhaps causing a battle, for the land/ heritage/inheritance of his grandfather. The question is: who was this grandfather? The traditional view is that it was Talorcan, which would mean that Bruide was fighting for all of Pictland, but more recent opinion reckons his maternal grandfather to have been a Pictish sub-king, as shown in illus.**1**. If this man was sub-king over the province of *Circinn* (Angus and Mearns), or even lord of Dunnichen, it would have great significance for the location of the battle. Alas, there is no way to tell.

The lack of any Pictish text relating to the Battle of Dunnichen may well be compensated for in the form of a dramatic narrative scene carved in stone. I refer to the famous Pictish symbol-stone now to be found in Aberlemno Churchyard, some four miles north of Dunnichen. The superb design and execution of the cross-side alone is sufficient to mark it as a piece of sculpture of the greatest merit, illustrating the high level of artistic and technical skill of the Pictish craftsmen. What concerns us here is the other side, which depicts a battle-scene unique in the field of Pictish art (**5**).

5 The battle-scene at Aberlemno *The symbol and narrative side of the Pictish cross-slab in Aberlemno Churchyard, Angus. Could the warlike scene depicted represent the Battle of Dunnichen?*

The battle-scene is composed of nine warriors, in three registers (containing two, four and three figures respectively). There is no division between them, and therefore no clear indication as to how this narrative is to be read. It may be regarded as a lithic snapshot of the battlefield, depicting one single scene; it may be seen as a composite illustration, in which case four separate incidents are portrayed; or it may represent a four-incident development of a single episode from the battle.

Five of the warriors are mounted, three are on foot, and one appears to be prostrate. Their separation into two warring armies of different cultures is indicated by those on the left being bareheaded and having pointed beards (these must surely be Picts, as they look very like many other figures seen on Pictish stones), while those on the right wear helmets with prominent nasals (surely not Picts, and considering that just such a helmet, dating to the 8th century, has been found in York, these must be Northumbrians). Two of the four incidents depict the rival forces in violent opposition; this is undoubtedly a battle-scene.

It is surmounted by two large symbols typical of the Pictish repertoire – the notched rectangle and Z-rod, and the triple disc. It is thought that these may be representations (stylised in the case of the first one) of a pony-chariot overlain by a twice-broken spear, and a ring-handled cauldron. There is no agreed version of the meaning of the Pictish symbols, but this pair could be interpreted as commemorating a deceased war-leader by means of a feast in honour of his memory. If so, it would seem reasonable to assume that he played an important part in the battle depicted below.

The narrative on the stone describes in dramatic visual terms an engagement in which Pictish infantry and cavalry, armed with swords, spears and round shields, encounter spear-wielding Northumbrian cavalry. The outcome is not in doubt: in the first incident, at the top, a Pictish horseman chases a Northumbrian horseman from the field, while in the final incident, at the bottom-right corner, a Northumbrian warrior lies prostrate, his corpse being pecked at by a carrion bird. This would have been readily understood at the time as a heroic motif indicating defeat in battle.

Contemporary literature is strewn with such references, in particular *Y Gododdin* (often cited as the oldest Scottish poem, though actually written in Brythonic Welsh), which was composed less than a century before the Battle of Dunnichen. It has a dozen references to dead warriors becoming food for carrion birds; phrases such as 'a raven's feast' and 'raven's gain' are metaphors for battle which resulted in heavy slaughter, while 'he was food for ravens' is an unequivocal statement that the warrior concerned had died in battle. That is what the final statement on the Aberlemno stone is saying: a Northumbrian (a large figure, and so presumably an important personage) lies dead, clearly implying that his side has been vanquished, leaving the Picts victorious.

Incidents two and three are most revealing, for they illustrate how the Picts employed clever tactics, in their use of both infantry and cavalry, to defeat their foe. (It is not appropriate to go into this in detail here; a separate volume dealing with this subject will soon be published.) If the Aberlemno stone bears a splendid representation of a Pictish army in battle (the only one), and if that Pictish army is shown defeating their arch-enemies the Northumbrians, then what better battle to commemorate in this way than their greatest victory, that won at Dunnichen. A persuasive argument can be made for dating the execution of the battle-scene very close to 685. The Picts have left us nothing in the way of written records of that momentous occasion; perhaps at Aberlemno they have bequeathed to us this compelling testimony in stone as a monument to their greatest triumph.

There is another form of record relating to the battle, though the degree of credence it is accorded is dependent upon one's views on supernatural powers. The battle has apparently inspired three visions, two of which occurred at the time, and the third more than twelve centuries later. The first two both relate to the death of Ecgfrith. Bishop Wilfrid was in Sussex at the time when the battle was fought. He was engaged in celebrating mass when he had a horrible vision of Ecgfrith falling forward with his head cut off. Two evil spirits then brought forward the spirit of the king, and bore it, sighing with a terrible groan, to the confines of Hell. However, this story first appears in the 'Life of St Wilfrid' by Eadmer, which was written more than four centuries after the battle, and he himself had doubts about its authenticity.

Much more immediate is the record of a similar vision experienced by Bishop Cuthbert, who was in Carlisle at the time of the battle. He had gone there to visit Ecgfrith's queen (Iurminburg, his second wife) who had arranged to await the outcome of the Pictish campaign at her sister's nunnery. While Cuthbert was on a conducted tour of the city walls, as he was being shown a remarkable fountain of Roman workmanship, he suddenly became troubled in spirit, and revealed that he had just seen the outcome of the battle, and that it had gone against the Northumbrians. He declined to give further details, but went directly to the queen and told her to expect the worst of news concerning the safety of her husband. Cuthbert was clearly dismayed at his vision, though he can hardly have been surprised at the content, for in an interview with Ecgfrith's sister, Abbess Aelfflaed, a year previously, he had prophesied the king's death at this time. Two days after the vision, the first Northumbrian survivor arrived at Carlisle, and confirmed events as Cuthbert had told them. This story is recorded in two versions of the 'Life of St Cuthbert', one by an anonymous monk of Lindisfarne about fifteen years later, the other by Bede some thirty-five years later.

The third reported vision occurred only in 1950, and concerns not the battle itself, but its aftermath. On a dark January night the story goes that Miss E.S. Smith was walking from the direction of Brechin to her home in the village of Letham when she saw moving figures holding torches coming from the direction of Dunnichen. Over a period of some twelve minutes she claimed to have experienced three different sightings – the first at a range of about a mile; the second much closer, the figures apparently skirting some now non-existent obstruction (its location would correspond with the north-east extension of the vanished mire), and the third at a distance of only fifty yards, which enabled her to detect details of the clothing and the torches. The task apparently being undertaken by these spectral figures, who were presumably Picts, was to identify their own dead among the corpses which littered the battlefield.

Opinion is divided as to the authenticity of this story. The feeling of the psychiatrist who interviewed Miss Smith and published the results was that she had experienced a genuine apparition while in an altered state of consciousness. However, he did allow for other possibilities, ranging from a genuinely-held but nonetheless false memory, to a hoax, or a fraud. It is the sort of story which enthusiastic historians would like to be able to believe, but for which there is not a shred of evidence, and it is only proper to view it with a degree of scepticism. At least this tale, and others concerning ghostly figures appearing when the mists are lying around Dunnichen, being caught in car headlights only to vanish an instant before the anticipated impact, demonstrate the level of feeling in the district for an event which happened so many centuries ago.

It is one of the disappointing features of the Battle of Dunnichen that so little now remains to be seen at the actual place. It seems reasonable to assume that Dun Nechtan occupied all or part of the low elliptical dome which crowns Dunnichen Hill, yet no obvious trace of it is apparent at the present time. There is a linear scatter of stones just below the summit plateau on the south side, below which is a terrace which looks as if it could be the result of the gradual erosion and collapse of an earthwork fortification such as a bank and internal ditch. An archaeological investigation could usefully be carried out to determine if this is the case. There is a major point of confusion, however, in that there appears to be a rival 'Dun Nechtan'. Most local writers mention that the remains of this ancient fort can still be seen, but its location is either ambiguous or it is placed quite definitely not on Dunnichen Hill but on nearby Castle Hill (or Cashel Hill).

The problem this poses is twofold: Castle Hill is such an insignificant eminence that it scarcely merits the name of 'hill' at all, and as such it is an unlikely situation for an ancient hill-fort; and it is to be found at some distance to the west, on the 'wrong' side of the hamlet of Dunnichen. However, it does have the benefit of possessing indications of the existence of some form of structure upon it. Ordnance Survey maps of the 19th century, bereft of any indication of historic remains on Dunnichen Hill, mark the 'site of tower' on Castle Hill, and a dense scatter of stones remains there to this day. Many are fragments, apparently coming from natural outcrops, and there is a tradition that the location was once a quarry. The 'tower', if it ever existed, would seem more likely to be medieval, though without proper investigation, it would be wrong to rule out the possibility of some more ancient structure having stood here. If that was Dun Nechtan, it would clearly have implications for the battle – the approach of the Northumbrians, the positioning of the Picts who sprang the ambush, and the battle site itself. In our present state of knowledge, Dun Nechtan is something of an enigma.

Although far from conclusive, the situation with regard to Nechtan's Mire is somewhat clearer. The only known representation of its extent before agricultural improvements reduced it in size appears on a map by John Ainslie of 1794 (**6**), where its outline appears similar to that

31

6 Ainslie's map of Angus   *This section of John Ainslie's 'Map of the County of Forfar or Shire of Angus' of 1794 includes the only known representation of Nechtan's Mire (unnamed, arrowed) before agricultural improvements reduced it in size. The mire is shown unchanged on the edition of 1801.*

suggested by Wainwright's later survey (**7**). Even before this date, drainage operations had begun. Ainslie did not name this feature, but maps of the 19th century (and of the 20th century, by which time the feature had vanished) call it Dunnichen Moss. Throughout the 19th century, field extensions relentlessly encroached upon it, reducing it to an irregular polygonal patch of rough pastureland, with a marshy core, and finally obliterating it from the landscape. In the early years of this century, part of the eastern section was a plantation, but eventually cultivated fields occupied the whole site. The spring which had fed the mire was bricked around and roofed over, and the water carried away by means of an underground conduit. A final remnant of the old mire still remained, however, lying just to the east of Dunnichen Church and its manse, at the bottom of the path running between them. This small parcel of marshy ground constituted the westernmost tip of Dunnichen Moss, and, by association, of Nechtan's Mire.

Occasionally, during a long spell of exceptionally wet weather, the mire has made efforts to re-establish itself, its erstwhile existence thereby achieving a modicum of transient realism. The ground lying at its central core has always been heavy under the plough even when not waterlogged, and eventually the farmer at East Mains of Dunnichen decided to rationalise his holding. In 1996, the marshy remnant near the kirk was finally obliterated, while at the same time the constant battle to cultivate the core was ended by allowing that area to lie under water once more. The ancient spring was released, field drains were laid running towards it, and a substantial pond created. It is inhabited by waterfowl, with ducks and water-hens regularly to be seen alongside less common visitors such as swans, and even – most appropriately – the occasional heron.

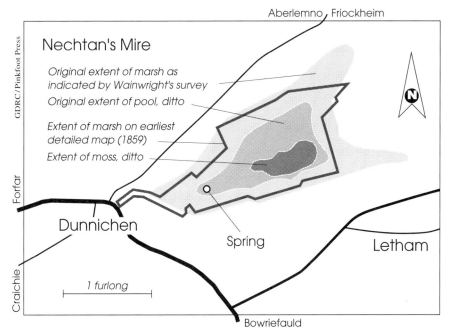

7 Nechtan's Mire reconstructed *A composite delineation of Nechtan's Mire (pool, marsh and moss) built up from map evidence and survey findings.*

5 Historiography of the Battle

The fragment of an enigmatic verse, a possible pictorial account in stone, three visions which it is impossible to substantiate – these are flimsy foundations upon which to construct the story of such an outstanding event as the Battle of Dunnichen. The trouble is, when we turn to primary historical sources, there is very little on offer. Only four sources can claim to be anything like contemporary; the sum total of information which they contain is meagre. The first historical mention of the battle comes about five years after the event, occurring in the 'Life of Columba' by Adamnan, written *circa* 690. However, it does not appear as a subject in its own right, but is merely used by Adamnan as a temporal reference point relating to his visit to Aldfrith (Ecgfrith's successor); the phrase simply reads 'after Ecgfrith's battle'.

The next reference to the battle occurs some ten years later, appearing in the 'Life of St Cuthbert' by an anonymous monk of Lindisfarne, written *circa* 700, though it relates not to the actual battle but to the vision which it generated. About 710, Eddius Stephanus wrote his 'Life of Bishop Wilfrid', and it contains a very poignant reference to the Battle of Dunnichen. He does not go into any detail, as he had done when recounting the previous Pictish-Northumbrian battle of *circa* 672 on the Plain of Manau, but he mentions the slaying of Ecgfrith 'and all the flower of his army' at the hands of the Picts, describing the event as 'a most woeful disaster'. Another version of the 'Life of St Cuthbert' was written by Bede *circa* 720, following his less-detailed metrical version, and again the reference is to Cuthbert's vision. However, Bede concludes with a very interesting sentence which is to be found nowhere else: 'The king was laid low by the sword of the enemy, and his bodyguard slain around him'.

We then come to the account of the battle given by Bede in his 'Ecclesiastical History of the English People', which he completed in 731. Annoyingly brief and incomplete it may be, but it is by far the most detailed and valuable historical source that exists. Using only phrases where sentences would have been so much more informative, Bede nonetheless contrives to describe Ecgfrith's attitude, the terrain he encountered, the Pictish tactics, the outcome of the conflict, the exact date, and the consequences of the Northumbrian defeat – rather more information than can be properly analysed within the confines of this booklet. On the latter topic, Bede offers by way of analogy a quotation from Virgil's 'Aeneid'. He says that from the time of the battle, the hopes and strength of the Northumbrian kingdom began *fluere ac retro sublapsa referri*. This phrase had been translated prosaically as 'to recede and sink', and rather more poetically as 'to backward flow and gliding fall away'. Bede is clearly indicating that defeat at Dunnichen initiated a period of Northumbrian decline, but why choose that particular phrase from the *Aeneid*? Just as Virgil blamed the desecration of the Palladium of Troy by the Greeks for their misfortunes, so Bede blamed the destruction of Irish churches and monasteries by Ecgfrith's troops in 684 as the reason for the disaster which overtook him in the following year. Bede saw the outcome of the battle, and indeed the whole Pictish campaign – in particular the king's rash decision to embark upon it – as divine retribution, pure and simple: 'The punishment for his sin was that he would not now listen to those who sought to save him from his own destruction'.

Even though he may have had mixed feelings about the fate of Ecgfrith, Bede can only have grieved over the catastrophe which overwhelmed the Northumbrian forces. This can be seen in his failure to give details, even important ones such as the name of the victorious Pictish king, and also in his final statement, regarding Aldfrith: 'He nobly restored the ruined state of the kingdom, though within narrower bounds'. This reads as if Bede was trying to put a brave face on what for him must have been a matter of personal sadness.

The next layer of historical record is not contemporary with the event, but gives the impression of drawing upon material which was. It is from the English chronicles and the Irish annals that we get the three names by which the battle may be known. The 'History of the Britons' by Nennius calls it *Gueith Linn Garan* – the Battle of the Pool of the Heron – as it was known to the Britons and perhaps even the Picts; the Irish annals favour *Cath Duin Neachtain* (with variations) – the Battle of Dun Nechtan – and their entries relating to Scotland seem to be based on a single compilation probably originating on Iona, which suggests this is how it was known to the Scots; and Symeon in his 'History of the Church of Durham' gives it the name *Nechtanesmere*. Of the three, the last is the only one which is not preceded by 'battle of'; instead, Symeon emphasises that the name applied to a topographical feature by immediately adding the qualifying phrase *quod est stagnum nechtani* – 'which is Nechtan's *stagnum*'. The last word is interesting, because it can mean standing water of various kinds: a pond, a swamp, or a marsh.

Most of these entries are brief, and consistent in the information they give – the year is generally omitted in preference for a relative sequence, but the date is precise: thirteen days before the kalends of June (*ie* 20th May); they agree that Ecgfrith was killed in his fortieth year, and in the fifteenth year of his reign. Only in a few instances are there to be found any snippets of information beyond this, such as the kinship of the leaders as mentioned by Nennius, or Bruide's title as king of *Fortriu* (Strathearn and Menteith) rather than of all Pictland, as stated by Tigernach. Only rarely can additional information be found in other sources, such as the vague location for the battle given in the 'Saxon Chronicle' – *be northan sae*. This has been translated simply as 'by the North Sea' (Dunnichen being only nine miles from the coast) or rather more complexly as 'benorth the sea', meaning 'to the north of an arm of the sea' (*ie* north of the Firth of Forth). Despite these later sources, most English medieval histories go back to Bede for their information, as does the only Scottish text of that period in which I have found mention of the great battle, 'The Chronicle of Holyrood'.

When coherent histories of Scotland came to be written, as opposed to the stilted method of compilation which resulted in the patchy chronicles, much the same line was followed. Bede appears as the only source, and the other ancient references seem to have been overlooked, forgotten, or unknown. The problem facing the authors of the early histories was that the narrative approach demanded from them a broader knowledge than the compilers of the chronicles possessed or at least had passed on. Such an important event for the development of the Scottish nation as the ending of Northumbrian expansion northwards had to be dealt with in an appropriate manner, and the reprehensible response seems to have been that where essential information was not available, then it should be invented.

Some writers shamelessly manipulated and falsified the evidence to suit their own ends. John of Fordun, writing in the 14th century, quotes

Bede as his source, but then blatantly changes 'province of the Picts' into 'province of the Scots', and credits the Scots with the victory! The situation deteriorated further in the 16th century with the history of Hector Boece, which not only sustains the myth of Ecgfrith's defeat representing a triumph for the Scots, but actually identifies its location as the banks of the River Lewis in Galloway (which would have put it in the territory of the Britons), which he claims was swollen by melting snow (on 20th May?!). Not only does Boece concoct a detailed and (it must be supposed) entirely fictitious account of the battle, but he introduces the Picts as allies of the Northumbrians, and makes them out to be spineless cowards with treasonable inclinations! The 18th century saw a saner approach, with historians content to follow Bede and ignore the fictitious inventions of their predecessors, but there were still occasional flights of fancy. Walter Goodall quotes Bede, and also Symeon of Durham, using the name of Nechtansmere, which he confidently places in Berwickshire.

The study of the Battle of Dunnichen as a historical event took a great step forward in 1807 with the publication of *Caledonia* by George Chalmers. For the first time, a historian made a serious attempt to reconstruct the path of Ecgfrith's invasion, and to select, by examination of the evidence and logical deduction, the actual site of the battle. Chalmers knew and used all the important ancient sources: Bede, Nennius, Symeon, the Annals of Ulster and of Tigernach, and the Saxon Chronicle, and he concluded: 'At length the two kings met at Nechtan's-mere, near Dun-Nechtan, the Dunnichen of the present day'. He went on to comment: 'Fruitless enquiries have hitherto been made for the true site of this important battle', and then listed, with comment but with limited quotation, the sources he had employed in solving the puzzle. This has led to Chalmers being hailed as the first scholar to associate Dun Nechtan with Dunnichen, but such a view is somewhat exaggerated. We cannot tell to what extent the notion may have been aired at antiquarian meetings, but at least one man went into print with such a thought at the end of the previous century when David MacPherson considered it, albeit unfavourably. The great strength of the work of George Chalmers was that he considered the problem as a historian, and produced a solution based upon historical reasoning.

While future historians would acknowledge their debt to George Chalmers in glowing terms, his identification of the battle-site was not greeted with universal acceptance, and, curiously, it was local people who seem to have been the strongest initial objectors. One was the minister of Dunnichen Parish, the Rev. James Headrick, who published a study of Angus six years later in 1813, in which he made no mention of the battle, but attacked the very cornerstone of Chalmers' reasoning by challenging the derivation of Dunnichen, favouring *Dun-Achan*, 'the fort of the valley' – as unlikely a military concept as an etymological deduction. This was also the view of a noted local antiquarian named James Thomson. In an unpublished manuscript of 1827, he expresses the view that it is futile to link Dunnichen with Nechtan's Mere because of the overt Englishness of the word 'mere'. In itself, that is a sensible argument; it is a pity that he was unaware of the 'Linn Garan' of Nennius.

The Rev. James Headrick returned to the fray in 1833 with his study of Dunnichen Parish in the *New Statistical Account*. He had to admit to a battle being fought in the vicinity, but he got in a terrible tangle trying to prevent it from being that of Dun Nechtan. He wrote: 'A confused tradition prevails of a great battle having been fought on the East Mains of Dunnichen', and he proceeded to confuse it further by stating the conflict to have been between the Picts and the Britons, ascribing to the Picts the wrong king (Lothus) and to the Britons none less than King Arthur, claiming that Dunnichen was where that 'hero of romance was slain'! Despite all the confusion and opposition, however, Chalmers' identification gained widespread acceptance.

Now Scottish historians had something more than a vague tradition to draw upon, and the importance of the battle could be writ large in the story of the emergent nation – though why the name Nechtansmere should have been commonly used, rather than either of the two more appropriate names, is something of a mystery. Now that it had been given a real sense of identity, writers felt free to eulogise its crucial significance, and some stirring lines were to grace the textbooks on early Scottish history. William Robertson in *Scotland under her Early Kings* (1862): 'The victory was as glorious as its consequences were important'. Alexander Philip in *The Picts in Angus* (1925): 'Ecgfrith was defeated and killed at Dunnichen, an important battle which may be said to have decided that Scotland should never become a province of England'. Agnes Muir Mackenzie in *The Foundations of Scotland* (1938): 'Nechtansmere is one of the most important battles in British history, for had its result chanced to go

8 Wainwright's survey, 1947 *One of the original photographs used by Frederick Wainwright to plot the extent of Nechtan's Mire. Looking south over East Mains of Dunnichen.*

otherwise, the Northumbrian power might have run to the Moray Firth, and the kingdom of Scotland never have existed'.

Such high-flying rhetoric helped to make up for the centuries of neglect, but curiously it did not stimulate any scholarly examination of the subject. Instead, authors gave the appearance of trying to outdo one another in the extravagance of their language. Some poured out emotion-charged prose, laden with hyperbole, while others were tempted beyond the point of discretion into developing fictitious accounts of the conflict with all the conviction of war correspondents reporting direct from the front. What the subject badly needed was for a historian of merit and repute to re-examine the sources and reassess the significance of the Battle of Dunnichen. Enter Frederick Wainwright.

Dr F.T. Wainwright was Head of the History Department of University College, Dundee, after the Second World War. The stimulus to his detailed study of the battle appears to have occurred in a curious and somewhat dramatic fashion, stemming not from a documentary discovery or an academic debate, but – the weather. As a result of flooding at the end of the winter of 1946–47, at least part of the old Nechtan's Mire was restored for a time. In the summer of 1947, after the water had departed, the flood-marks were still visible in the fields. Wainwright must already have been familiar with the basic history of the battle and the accepted location of Nechtan's Mire, and it seems that the temporary revival of this vanished feature provided him with the necessary impetus to undertake a thorough study of the subject.

The work of Frederick Wainwright is extremely valuable in three respects. Firstly, he gathered, quoted, and analysed the principal elements of the ancient sources, thus allowing a history of the battle to be constructed which was at least coherent, if not comprehensive. Secondly, he conducted a field-survey, the results of which enabled him to plot the likely perimeter of the ancient mire (**8**). Considering that this feature was taken by the Britons (and Picts?) and the English to give the battle its name, its delineation on a map added a touch of current reality to distant history. Finally, Wainwright made a calculated assessment of the campaign and its consequences, and the studied conclusions which he drew were apparently designed to offset the more exaggerated claims which he felt had been made by earlier historians. The results of this study were published in the magazine *Antiquity* in 1948. That article constitutes not only the most detailed examination of the Battle of Dunnichen by any historian up to that time, but also a valuable contribution to the history of the Picts and of the formation of the Scottish nation.

The name of 'Nechtansmere' was now at the pen-tip of every Scottish historical writer, and very few modern Scottish histories fail to include a mention of the battle. However, most of these vary between brief and very brief, and it may be considered rather curious that such a small number deal with the subject in any detail. Frederick Wainwright himself devoted several paragraphs to the battle in the chapter which he wrote in the book which he edited – *The Problem of the Picts* (1955). Isabel Henderson did likewise in her standard work *The Picts* (1967). Peter Marren produced a creditable summary for the general reader in the Aberdeen *Leopard* magazine of May 1982. Beyond these, there was not much of substance. Occasional articles in learned journals and volumes of collected essays consider related topics such as the accounts of Bede and Nennius, and the victory song, but there was no systematic and comprehensive review of the Battle of Dunnichen, and its importance.

A fresh appraisal of this ancient event was long overdue, and so the Forfar and District Historical Society took advantage of the occasion of the battle's 1300th anniversary and invited the present author to address them on the subject in the Meffan Institute, Forfar, on 4th March 1985, and to write a booklet about it, which was published on 25th May 1985, on which this present volume is based.

6 Dunnichen – a Place in History

When the Battle of Dunnichen has achieved its rightful place among the great and decisive battles of Scotland, recognised as such by both historians and the public, how will it be presented as an important element in our national history? Hopefully, it will be accorded a fuller and more appropriate treatment in history textbooks, where its significance will receive adequate explanation. As to the battlefield site itself, will it become a revered place of pilgrimage, as is now the case with Bannockburn and Culloden?

Proper recognition of the importance of the Battle of Dunnichen is moving onto a more appropriate level, but only slowly. The occasion of its 1300th anniversary in 1985 certainly provided great impetus to such a movement, with the staging of lectures and battlefield addresses, radio and television presentations, and the publication of articles, a pamphlet, and a booklet (most of which this author was involved with). Two commemorative postal covers were also issued, and the Society of Antiquaries of Scotland chose Dunnichen as the venue for their annual excursion. Perhaps the most permanent contribution to the celebrations was the erection of a commemorative cairn at Dunnichen, under the auspices of the Letham and District Community Council, which acts as a focal point for those visiting the battle-site. In addition to countless informal visits, this has now become a regular event with some organisations, such as the Pictish Arts Society when celebrating Dunnichen Day, and the 'Stones of the Picts' course which the writer conducts for Edinburgh University's Open Studies programme (**9**).

Despite all these events, and the publicity surrounding them, recognition of the proper place of the Battle of Dunnichen has still not achieved the status it deserves. In 1988, the *Sunday Mail* launched a weekly magazine, issued in 52 parts, entitled 'The Story of Scotland', but no mention whatever of the battle appeared. The same total omission occurs in the book *The Story of Scotland* by the well-known historical novelist Nigel Tranter, published in 1987; in a piece of unscholarly writing about the Picts, he makes no reference at all to the battle. Completely

9 The memorial cairn at Dunnichen *The author (second from right) pictured with some members of his course 'Stones of the Picts', at the memorial cairn on Dunnichen Green, in 1991.*

ignoring the event is bad enough, but even worse was to come in the volume on 'Angus and the Mearns' in the *Discovering* series produced by John Donald Publishers, dealing with various areas of Scotland, which appeared in 1990. The author, I. Henderson of Brechin, employs a combination of factual inaccuracy and distortion to denigrate the Dunnichen episode and its adherents in a shameful and unjustifiable manner. The spirit of the rascally James Headrick lives on, it would seem, and some work still remains to be done to convince all interested parties, both local and national, of the importance of Dunnichen in Scottish history. At least the subject is given a worthy treatment by Peter Marren in his fine book *Grampian Battlefields* (1990).

A threat of a different and far more damaging nature occurred in May 1991, when Laird Brothers of Lunanhead (just outside Forfar and only three miles from Dunnichen) applied for planning permission to open a quarry on West Dunnichen Hill. The implementation of their plan to remove some 4.5 million tonnes of hard rock (andesitic basalt) over a thirty-year period would have destroyed the visual explanation for king

Bruide's battle strategy, and would have had a devastating effect on our ability to appreciate such a concept. While the Planning and Development Committee of Angus District Council was considering the application, local opinion united strongly against the plans. The 'Save Dunnichen Hill' campaign, co-ordinated by Scott Kidd of Letham, argued forcefully for the rejection of the proposals from a number of standpoints, one being historical, and national authorities added their support. At the height of the debate, Geoffrey Barrow (formerly Professor of Scottish History at Edinburgh University) said in *The Scotsman* that the Battle of Dunnichen 'ranks alongside Bannockburn in importance', and no-one who has studied the subject would disagree with that opinion. Hundreds of letters of protest poured in from all parts of Scotland and many far-distant places. Faced with such overwhelming opposition, Laird Brothers withdrew their application, though they still own the land, and the long-term preservation of Dunnichen Hill and the vicinity of the battle-site is a matter still to be resolved.

It might be an exaggeration to say that the Battle of Dunnichen created Scotland, but it is no exaggeration to say that it created the circumstances which allowed the embryo Scottish nation to materialise and to grow to maturity. The converse is equally true: had it not been for this battle, or had the Picts not been the victors, there may well never have been a Scottish nation. All those Scots who take a pride in their native land should look with gratitude upon the Picts, upon the inspirational leadership of king Bruide, and upon the events which occurred more than thirteen centuries ago at Dunnichen.

mc Oᵿᴧ ᴨ1 Saxan

Appendix   The Dunnichen Stone

Although no tangible remains of the Battle of Dunnichen have been discovered, there is one Pictish artefact which has direct associations with the locality: a large stone bearing Pictish symbols (**10**). No accurate report exists of its discovery, but it is said to have been dug up somewhere on the Dunnichen estate in 1805, and in time it was erected in the grounds of Dunnichen House. It naturally assumed the name 'The Dunnichen Stone', and became much admired as being an extremely fine example of this class of Pictish art.

The Dunnichen Stone is a large, irregular block of sandstone standing over four feet high, being some two feet wide and one foot thick. Its surface is naturally rough, apart from one face which may have been artificially smoothed, and this bears three Pictish symbols. They are executed by linear incision, and thus no part of the design appears in relief. Although the technique of execution is hardly sophisticated, the proportions of the different elements and the command of line displayed by the sculptor exhibit a high degree of artistic appreciation.

There is no general agreement on what the various Pictish symbols are intended to illustrate – the full range consists of upwards of fifty symbols – and theories abound (none of which can be substantiated) on their actual meaning. Apart from their obvious intrinsic beauty, they would seem to comprise a series of pictograms, which appear in various combinations in order to express a variety of stereotyped messages. Beyond that, all is speculation. Reading from the top, the symbols on the Dunnichen Stone may be regarded as follows:

1 The 'flower' symbol
This is one of the least common of the Pictish symbols ; it is probably stylised, and may be totally abstract. It has long been known as the 'flower' symbol, presumably because the two curving tendrils may be thought of as stamens, but the rest of it hardly looks botanical. One fanciful interpretation seeks to link it with the animal on the Rhynie Stone no.5,

Graeme Cruickshank

10 The Dunnichen Stone   *Shown here (scale in inches) at its former site in the garden of Dunnichen House in 1967. It is currently on display at the Meffan Institute, Forfar.*

46

which may be the top half of an otter, seeing in this design the bottom half of the animal caught in the act of diving! More realistically, it has been regarded as an item of chariotry or equestrian gear, possibly a harness-brooch (belonging to a time prior to the advent of the historical Picts), but no direct prototype has been discovered, as with several other artefacts which feature in the panoply of Pictish symbols. The 'flower' name continues to persist, however, and it may possibly be a tribal emblem. The Dunnichen example is widely reckoned to be the prime version of this particular symbol.

2 The double-disc and Z-rod

The double-disc would seem to be a purely abstract symbol (it is certainly not a dumbbell, as it is sometimes termed), while attempts to promote it as showing the sun and moon linked together are entirely speculative. The Z-rod, with which the symbol is generally associated, would appear to be used as a qualifier, as it never occurs alone (and it only occurs with two other symbols). It may be a twice-broken spear (just as the V-rod, which is generally associated with the crescent symbol, and likewise never appears alone, may be a once-broken arrow). In some cultures, the burial of a leader or person of high status is accompanied by a ceremony in which his weapons are broken and cast into the grave. Perhaps the Z-rod, and V-rod, are used adjectivally to signify 'dead', and as only four symbols are qualified in this way, they may represent very senior ranks of society. One theory suggests that the double-disc implies kingship. As seen on the Dunnichen Stone, the internal whorl decoration of the discs, and the rendition of the barbs and flights on the spear (if that is what they are), are unmatched for the beauty and balance of their curved lines compared with any other version of this symbol, which is relatively common in Pictish art.

3 The mirror and comb

There is general agreement that these are truly representational symbols. The comb (a number of bone examples of which have been recovered by archaeology) is here rather plain; frequently the top is ornamented, or there are two rows of teeth making it double-sided. The mirror (of polished bronze in its real form) also appears to be very plain; normally the handle was intricate and artistic. No example of a Pictish mirror is known, and it is reckoned that this symbol derives from Brigantian examples of the Insular La Tène type being traded north over Hadrian's Wall – another category of metal object which would appear to predate the historical Picts.

The mirror is generally accompanied by the comb, as at Dunnichen, though the comb never appears alone; thus the mirror and comb may be perceived as a single symbol. It usually occurs at the end of the statement, and therefore may be regarded as a stereotyped addition to the basic message. If these stones are memorials (though not necessarily grave-markers), and especially if the broken weapon indicates that the person commemorated is deceased, then the mirror and comb could indicate a category of person at whose instigation the memorial had been erected. One theory sees this as representing a woman, a mirror and comb being regarded as essentially feminine accoutrements, necessary for the care of long tresses, who might therefore be the wife of the important man thus commemorated. However, against this, the many examples of Pictish men illustrated on standing stones generally show them to have long, flowing hair and pointed beards, and thus it could be argued that a mirror and comb would have been just as important to a man. Perhaps this symbol indicates the personal attendant (valet) of a high-ranking man, himself of some social standing, whose final duty to his dead master was to oversee the erection of his memorial.

Taken together, these three symbols conveyed a message to the Picts of that time. There have been a number of weird and fanciful interpretations of the Dunnichen symbols, as indicated by the anonymous 'P.C.' (surely not Patrick Chalmers?) in 1848 in a treatise, *The Sculptured Stones of Angus*: 'One of the figures has been described as representing the head and shoulders of a man in armour; others have supposed it to be the cap of Osiris surmounted by the flower of the lotus.' Perhaps, on the basis of the preceding paragraphs, a more appropriate interpretation can be deduced. The symbolic message may possibly read as follows:

Erected to commemorate the deceased king of
the Flower tribe, by his personal attendant.

The Dunnichen Stone belongs to the Class I period of Pictish stone-cut art: it is a rough boulder, bearing incised designs, consisting of symbols only, cut on the most suitable flattish area. It is, indeed, 'pure' Class I, displaying no hint whatever of any of the characteristics of a Class

II stone, which is a dressed rectangular slab, bearing relief sculpture, consisting of the Christian cross and narrative scenes in addition to symbols, on both sides. The Dunnichen Stone thus falls into the very earliest period of Pictish stone-cut art. Applying a date to this is not easy because of the lack of dateable evidence, but sometime around the 5th/6th century seems most likely. This unfortunately places the Dunnichen Stone rather too early to claim any association with the great battle of 685, though such a link should not be totally discounted.

Since its discovery in 1805, the Dunnichen Stone has had a rather chequered history. At some stage during post-Pictish times, two vertical lines were cut deep into the stone, presumably in a misguided effort to regularise its shape. Fortunately, the scheme was not carried to fruition, and although some damage was done to the symbols, notably the right-hand disc, the basic outline of the stone has remained intact.

For some time after its discovery, the stone apparently lay neglected. It was first erected at the Kirkton, and then moved a short distance into the gardens of Dunnichen House around the turn of the 19th century. There it proudly stood in a commanding position for seventy years or so, until the Dunnichen estate passed into the hands of the Colefax family of Newbury in Berkshire. Dunnichen House was demolished, the grounds were turned into a market garden, and the future of the stone became uncertain. The Department of the Environment took charge of the stone with the intention of adding it to the collection of Pictish stones in their museum at St Vigeans. Pending its installation there, it was stored nearby at Arbroath Abbey, but the plan was not carried through. Instead, the stone was acquired by Dundee City Museums, which had assumed a regional interest in addition to civic responsibilities, prior to the creation of Angus District Museums. It went on display at the main Dundee Museum in Albert Square in 1972 (although it does not appear to have been entered into the accessions register until 1978, and ownership of the stone was not granted to Dundee Museum until 1991, almost twenty years after its acquisition).

The move to Dundee was to prove somewhat controversial. The local people did not appreciate their principal antiquity, by now well known and much admired, being removed from the locality, especially when it became known that its new home was in a city-centre museum, inevitably lacking any of the character of its original environment. Almost immediately, amid claims that its removal had been improper, there were demands for its return to Dunnichen. Suggestions that it was suffering from the effects of weathering were countered by a proposal to construct a shelter to accommodate it there. In 1973, the cause was taken up by the Convener of Angus County Council, who made strenuous efforts to secure the reinstatement of the stone at Dunnichen. Such moves were repeated at the time of local government reorganisation in 1975, though without success.

With the authorities deadlocked, a compromise was agreed, and in 1977 a fibreglass replica was placed on Dunnichen Green. It was made by James Henderson of Arbroath with the co-operation of Dundee Museum, and was erected by Letham and District Community Council and Forfar and District Historical Society, a leading figure being Sheriff Stuart Kermack. While this move was appreciated, there remained a strong local feeling that the original should have been reinstated, with Dundee Museum retaining the replica. It became evident that there was a serious question mark over whether the Dunnichen Stone had found its final resting place.

A possible compromise emerged in the shape of the Meffan Institute in Forfar, which housed the Local History museum for the Forfar area, and its refurbishment in the early 1990s, encompassing a Pictish element for the first time, made it a realistic contender as a home for the Dunnichen Stone. As had been the case two decades earlier, the local government reorganisation of 1996 provided another platform for negotiation.

The debate was now more public than ever, with a spate of articles in local newspapers highlighting what was being described as a tug-of-war between the two councils involved, Angus and Dundee. It seemed that intransigence would throttle any chance of relocation for the Dunnichen Stone, when suddenly the climate of hostility thawed, agreement was reached, and the stone was transferred to the Meffan in February 1997 on long-term loan. The move was greeted with delight by local people and hailed as a triumph by the local press. Now the Dunnichen Stone may be viewed not much more than three miles from the finding-place and likely point of origin of this prime example of a Pictish Class I stone, which, notwithstanding the greater sophistication of later Pictish sculptors, represents one of the highest achievements of Pictish stone-cut art.

Further Reading

First detailed appraisal:
Wainwright, Frederick 'Nechtanesmere' (*Antiquity*, vol XXII, 1948).

In summary form:
Cruickshank, Graeme 'The Battle of Nechtansmere' (Heritage Society of Scotland, pamphlet inserted into commemorative postal cover issued on 20th May 1985, the 1300th anniversary of the Battle).

Cruickshank, Graeme 'Forgotten conflict that changed the course of Scottish history' (*The Weekend Scotsman,* 25th May 1985; issued to coincide with the 1300th anniversary celebrations).

Cruickshank, Graeme 'Nechtansmere 685' (*Scottish Ambassador*, No.2, Winter 1986).

Refuting derogatory assertions:
Cruickshank, Graeme 'Moonshine on Dunnichen' (*Pictish Arts Society Newsletter,* No.9, Winter 1991).

In somewhat fuller form:
Marren, Peter 'Nechtansmere', chapter 2 in his book *Grampian Battlefields* (Aberdeen, 1990).

Suggesting alternative location:
Alcock, Leslie 'The Site of the Battle of Dunnichen' (*Scottish Historical Review*, vol LXXV, 1996).

Developing the Dunnichen/Aberlemno link:
Cruickshank, Graeme 'The Battle of Dunnichen and the Aberlemno Battle-Scene', a chapter in the book *Alba: Celtic Scotland in the Medieval Era* (ed. Edward Cowan), publication forthcoming.

Considering what the Battle should be called:
Cruickshank, Graeme 'The Battle of Dunnichen: whose name is it anyway?' (*Scottish Local History Journal,* forthcoming).

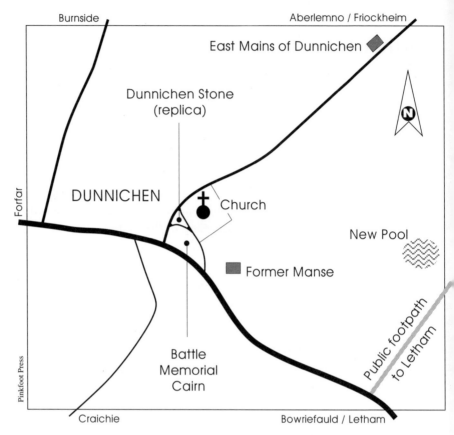

Burnside

Aberlemno / Friockheim

East Mains of Dunnichen

Dunnichen Stone
(replica)

N

Forfar

DUNNICHEN

Church

New Pool

Former Manse

Public footpath
to Letham

Pinkfoot Press

Battle
Memorial
Cairn

Craichie

Bowriefauld / Letham

11 Dunnichen today *Access to the Dunnichen Stone replica and memorial cairn is at all times, and cars can be parked in the loop off the main road. The modern pond is on private farm land and not accessible, but can be viewed from a short distance along the road which runs behind the kirk. One of the best ways to appreciate the whole area is by a gentle circular walk of nearly three miles. The route follows the road down past the manse then along the signposted public footpath to Letham. For part of its length, this mown track runs alongside the former Dunnichen Moss (Nechtan's Mire), and from the memorial to Scott Kidd there are splendid views across the new pond and up to the summit of Dunnichen Hill. At Letham Village Hall the route goes north up Auldbar Road by Drummietermont and the 'Girdle Stane', a prehistoric cup-and-ring-marked stone which is now prominently displayed at the roadside. Shortly after this, the route runs west back to Dunnichen passing East Mains, whose land comprises roughly the area of the battle-site. A different perspective can be had by taking the steep public road running from the entrance to Dunnichen House to Burnside over the saddle between East and West Dunnichen Hills, affording extensive views down over the whole area.* DH